Listening to the Spirit

Listening
to
the
spirit

Prayers for All Occasions

John E. Biegert

UNITED CHURCH PRESS · CLEVELAND, OHIO

United Church Press, Cleveland, Ohio 44115
© 1996 by John E. Biegert

Biblical quotations are from the New Revised Standard Version of the Bible
© 1989 by the Division of Christian Education of the National Council of the
Churches of Christ in the U.S.A., and are used by permission

Printed in the United States of America on acid-free paper
01   00   99   98   97   96   5   4   3   2   1

Library of Congress Cataloging-in-Publication Data

Biegert, John E.
    Listening to the Spirit : prayers for all occasions / John E.
Biegert.
        p.   cm.
    ISBN 0-8298-1075-7 (alk. paper)
    1. Prayers. I. Title.
BV245.B549   1996   95-51674
242'.8—dc20   CIP

To my wife Evelyn, daughter Diane, son Douglas and his family, and the members of First Congregational Church (United Church of Christ) of LaGrange, Illinois, who shared in the shaping and praying of these prayers

Contents

Prayers upon Awakening

God of this new day and every day, for the rest and sleep that I have experienced, for the gifts of yesterday, and for the potential and possibilities of today, accept my thanks. Awaken me once again to your presence within and around me, and may I seek to use wisely the hours that lie before me. May the words that come from my lips and the actions that stem from my hands and mind reflect my heartfelt resolve to live and love as did Jesus who is the light of the world, the Christ, in whose spirit I pray. Amen.

To you, O God, who separates the light from the shadows, I offer my gratitude for the dawn of this new day. Forgive me for what I did or neglected to do yesterday that failed to reflect your will. Strengthen my sensitivity to the needs of those whom I will meet in these coming hours, and may my life brighten the way of all whose paths cross mine. Amen.

Creator God, who in the past has been my refuge and strength and the One in whom I have put my trust, may I continue to be aware of your love and presence throughout this new day. Since I am not perfect, as I go about today's tasks deliver me when I despair, fortify me when I fail, humble me when I become haughty, love me when I lose, sustain me when I slip, save me when I sin. Thus surrounded and undergirded by your Spirit, enable me to cope with whatever comes my way. Amen.

Thank you, living and loving God, for the gift of this new day! As my eyes open and refocus, as the muscles of my body stretch and resume functioning, as my mind begins to reflect on the activities and opportunities that await me in the coming hours, I realize once again just how precious life is and how grateful I am to be alive. Yes, thank you, gracious and giving God, for this new day! Amen.

It's morning, O God, although it is difficult to discern because the day is so dark and dreary. The rain pelting my windows makes me want to crawl back into bed, pull the covers over my head, and wait for the sun to break through the clouds. But, O God, may the rain remind me of the blessings that you shower on my life. For family, for friends, for food, for faith, for forgiveness, for fortitude, thank you! Amen.

God of light and sun, God of this and every day: before beginning the tasks, confronting the challenges, and enjoying the opportunities that lie before me in the coming hours, enable me to center and focus my life on you, the Source and Ground of my Being. As I move through this day may the decisions I make reflect who and whose I am. May I, like the psalmist, affirm that you are my God and I am one of the people of your pasture and the sheep of your hand. Thus, I offer my prayer and desire to live this day in the spirit of the one who is the Good Shepherd—Jesus, the Christ. Amen.

Gracious and guiding God, who has given me a mentor and example for living in Jesus, I pray that you will give me the courage and will to see more clearly, love more dearly, and follow more nearly the Christ, day by day. Today, therefore, may I be sensitive to the needs of others and in some way respond to them; may I be kind and loving in all that I do and say; and may I reflect the image and spirit of Jesus who was called "The One for Others" because he sought to serve rather than to be served. Amen.

Prayers before Mealtime

Bountiful God, who has blessed us beyond our comprehension, accept our thanks for the food we are about to eat. As it nourishes our bodies, may we remember that our spirits are nourished by the one who said, "I am the bread of life. Whoever comes to me will never be hungry, and whoever believes in me will never be thirsty." Amen.

Holy One, we pause before breaking bread together to remember who and whose we are. For taking for granted what we have been given, for forgetting that life is a gift to be used wisely and not wasted, forgive us. May this food strengthen our bodies and our communal feeling around this table enrich our lives. Amen.

God, our Creator and Source of our strength, be our unseen guest at this table. For the gift of a world in which food can be grown and water obtained, thank you. Bless all who have been a part of the chain that has resulted in what is spread before us, and bless especially the one whose hands have prepared it. Amen.

Eternal God of all, as we pause at this table laden with food and drink, we remember your children, our sisters and brothers, whose lives ache from hunger and thirst at this moment. Move us to compassion for those less fortunate than we, and may we this day show our love for you by giving to some group or agency that is helping to feed the hungry and quench the thirst of the thirsty. We pray in the spirit of Jesus, who taught, "As you did it to one of the least of these who are members of my family, you did it to me." Amen.

Great and gracious God, we thank you for what we are about to eat. But even as our physical hunger is satisfied, may we not forget Jesus' words, "One does not live by bread alone." Thus, may we also fill our lives this day with times in which we read from your Word and meditate on your love for us and your will for our lives. Amen.

Giver of every good and perfect gift, God of the universe and our God: for life, for health, for family, friends, and food, we thank you. The hunger of our bodies will be satisfied by the food we are about to eat. But may our thirst for right living never be quenched. For we remember the words of and pray in the spirit of Jesus, who said, "Happy are those who hunger and thirst for righteousness, for they shall be filled." Amen.

As we gather around this table laden with the bounty of the earth, we are mindful, O God, of all that we have and how richly our lives have been blessed. May the gifts we have been given remind us that we are stewards of life, not owners. Thus, may we use our time, talents, and resources to further your will and ways. Amen.

Prayers before Bedtime

As the shades of night draw around me and darkness enfolds me, as my body and mind prepare for a few hours of rest and refreshment, I pause to thank you, Inexhaustible God, for the blessings of this day. For life itself, for the people with whom I have shared this day, and for your presence within me, thank you. May I express my gratitude for not having to walk alone by being there for someone else tomorrow. Amen.

It has been a long day, and I am tired and ready for bed, O God. The fact that you are tireless, timeless, ever-present, ever-giving, ever-gracious, and ever-loving reminds me anew that you are my God and I am a finite being who relies on you, the Source of my Being. As I close my eyes and relax the tense muscles of my body, as I place in your loving care the worries and concerns that have been mine this day, grant me sleep so that I will awaken in the morning strengthened and renewed to face the challenges and opportunities of tomorrow. Amen.

God of all times and places; God of the day and night; God of the sun, moon, and stars; and my God; I offer my gratitude for the gift of this day now drawing to its close. For the good experiences that were mine, for the pleasures found in unexpected places, and for the opportunities to serve you by serving others, accept my thanks. But, gracious God, I confess that I did and said what I should not have, and I left undone much that I might have said and done. Forgive me, and in your mercy strengthen me to be a better person tomorrow than I was today. Amen.

O God, my help in ages past and my hope for years to come, before sleep concludes this page in my book of life, I want to reflect on what I have written today. As I do so I find that I like much that I read, but there are some lines I wish were not there. Forgive me for those, merciful God. Trusting in your forgiving love, enable me to say with your apostle Paul, "Forgetting what lies behind and straining forward to what lies ahead, I press on toward the goal for the prize of the upward call of God in Christ Jesus." In his spirit I pray. Amen.

Guardian of my life, who blessed me with the gift of another day, I praise you as did the psalmists who sang, "I will bless God at all times; God's praise shall continually be on my mouth. . . . I sought God and God answered me, and delivered me from all my fears." "Where can I go from your spirit? Or where can I flee from your presence? If I ascend to heaven, you are there; if I make my bed in Sheol, you are there. If I take the wings of the morning and settle at the farthest limits of the sea, even there your hand shall lead me, and your right hand shall hold me fast." In this knowledge and assurance, grant me a restful sleep, and may I awake refreshed and strengthened to serve you by loving and serving others. Amen.

Spirit of the living God, fall afresh on me as I prepare for a time of rest from the labors of this day. Guard me throughout the night so that I might feel renewed and have a deepened resolve to live tomorrow as you would have me live. Amen.

O God, my Eternal Contemporary, whom I love because you first loved me, as this day dies and the blessing of rest awaits me, my thoughts and prayers turn to those I love and whom I know love me. For all of the ways in which they have brought me joy, satisfaction, and fulfillment, thank you! Because the love we share is so important to me, beginning tomorrow may I say each day to at least one of my loved ones, "I love you." May my verbal or written contact with those I love reveal that for me love is a verb. I pray in the spirit of Jesus, whose life and teachings show me how to love. Amen.

Prayers of Gratitude

Ever-giving and generous God, who loves me not because of my merits but just because I am; I pause in your presence, overwhelmed by the blessings that are mine. Life itself, family, friends, food, home, church, community, the marvels and beauty of creation, and other blessings too numerous to mention fill my life to overflowing. Keep me, I pray, from ever taking for granted what I enjoy. And may I always remember that I am the caregiver and caretaker, not the owner, of all that seems to be mine. In gratitude and humility I pray. Amen.

Caring Creator, whose love surrounds me, whose strength supports me, whose truth enlightens me, and whose spirit leads me; you have given me an example and pattern for my daily living in Jesus, the Christ. For his life and teachings, for his showing me the way, and for his revelation that you are always with me, I offer my heartfelt thanks. May my actions and my attitudes reflect my gratitude! Amen.

O Eternal Contemporary, whom I have come to know and love through the marvels and beauty of your creation; through your child Jesus, the Christ; and through your ever-present and empowering Holy Spirit: thank you for being a God who is not only beyond me but also within me; a God who cannot spare me from life but who can and will help me through life; and a God who loves

me just as I am. May my gratitude be expressed as I seek
to make my actions consistent with the faith I feel in my
heart and profess with my lips. Amen.

Loving God, my Comforter when I am comfortless, my
Friend when I am friendless, my Healer when I am hurting, my Helper when I feel helpless, my Hope when I am
hopeless, my Salvation when I sin; you who are caring
when I am careless, compassionate when I am compas-
sionless, faithful when I am faithless, merciful when I
am merciless: how great you are! Thank you for loving
me even when I am unlovable and for walking with me
each step of life's way. With my heart filled with gratitude I sing with the psalmist: "Bless God, O my soul,
and all that is within me, bless God's holy name. Bless
God, O my soul, and do not forget all God's benefits."
Amen.

Persuasive Presence, who loves and cares for me as a
shepherd loves and cares for the flock, awaken me anew
to your presence within and around me. You seek me
when I go astray; you pick me up when I fall; you carry
me when I am weak; you love me when I am unlovable.
For your unmerited love and amazing grace I praise your
name and express my heartfelt gratitude. Amen.

Eternal God, whose mercy encompasses the universe and
whose love embraces all humankind, as a part of your
creation in this time and place I pause to praise you for

the world in which I live and for all of the blessings that I enjoy. To reflect my gratitude, I rededicate myself to loving people and using things rather than loving things and using people. For every human being is your child and thus my sister or brother. Amen.

Prayers for Forgiveness

Faithful and forgiving God, who loves me as I am as well as for whom I can become, who sees through my problems and envisions my potential; thank you for enabling me both to be and to become. For my past and present sins of commission and omission, I ask your pardon. Enabled by your amazing grace, may I become more the person you want me to be. Amen.

Righteous God, I confess that in your presence and among your other children I have sinned in thought, word, and deed. Like Paul of old, "I do not understand my own actions. For I do not do what I want, but I do the very thing I hate." But you, compassionate God, are like a merciful mother or a forgiving father who is more willing to accept and love me than I am willing to accept and love myself. You desire to build me up even as I continue to tear myself down. In these moments may your love so penetrate my hard heart that I will not self-destruct but begin to be rebuilt by the power of your ever-present and empowering Holy Spirit. Amen.

Patient, persistent, and pursuing God, whose still, small voice calls me again and again to move from death to life—that is, from faithlessness to faithfulness, from selfishness to generosity, from grudge bearing to forgiving, from living in the past to embracing the present—forgive my stubbornness and for being so slow to respond to you.

May the gentle breath of your spirit so refresh and renew every part of my being that my hands better will serve you, my lips more often praise you, and my heart more consistently love you. Thus, may I become more like Jesus, in whose spirit I pray. Amen.

Loving God, who continually invites me to accept your guiding grace, forgive me for the times when I have turned my back on you. May I be inspired to say "yes" to your will and ways so that I will become more the person you want me to be—one who seeks to emulate Jesus, the Christ, in whose spirit I pray. Amen.

Prayers for Guidance and Help

Concerned and caring God, how much I need the assurance of your presence and help. I am tired and discouraged. I feel weighted down by the burdens of my life. So inscribe within my heart the words of your prophet: "Have you not known? Have you not heard? God is the everlasting God, the Creator of the ends of the earth. God does not faint or grow weary; God's understanding is unsearchable. God gives power to the faint, and strengthens the powerless. Even youths will faint and be weary, and the young will fall exhausted; but those who wait for God shall renew their strength, they shall mount up with wings like eagles, they shall run and not be weary, they shall walk and not faint." Mindful of this promise, I now can deal with this day! Amen.

Great God of Hope, I pause before you because I know that you will hear my prayer. At this difficult time in my life I need assurance because I am anxious, direction because I am drifting, energy because I feel empty, love because I feel lonely. Open my heart, Holy One, to the empowering and refreshing breath of your Spirit. Open my eyes, Enlightening One, to the paths I should take. For you, O God, are my refuge and strength, and a very present help in trouble. This I have learned especially through Jesus, the Christ, my Savior, in whose spirit I pray. Amen.

Great and Gracious God, who taught me through your child Jesus that I am to love you with my mind as well as my heart, soul, and strength; thank you for the privilege of asking, questioning, and even doubting what I have been taught. As I struggle with my faith, may I move ever closer to the truth which sets me free—the truth I experience in the one who is the Way, the Truth, and the Life, even Jesus, the Christ. Amen.

Prayers before Community Gatherings

O Holy One, whom we call by different names because we are a diverse people, but who has called us to live together in community, respecting the uniqueness and gifts of each and every person; grant your presence among us as we share in this significant occasion. Give us ears that hear one another, voices that speak the truth in love, minds that make sense out of confusion or disorder, and hearts that seek to fulfill your purposes. Amen.

Creator and creating God, you who have the whole world in your hands, we claim to be one nation, under you, and that you are the One in whom we trust. May the words we speak and the actions we take while we are together reflect what we profess. Amen.

Eternal Spirit of the universe, we gather as an organization committed to making our community, nation, and world better places in which to live. Bless us, we pray, as we meet this day. May our presence and participation inform, enrich, and inspire our lives and also challenge us anew to live out the principles and vision that we share in common. Amen.

God of our forebears, God of our mothers and fathers, and our God; we are mindful this day of the heritage left by those who founded and those who were a part of this community in years gone by. May we not take for granted what we have been given, and may we be responsible citizens who strive continually to make liberty and justice a reality for all. Amen.

Fountain of life, light, and truth, you have so created us that we realize in the depths of our beings that none of us is an island and that none of us wants to walk alone. We have experienced that our hearts are restless until they rest in you and in one another. Therefore, we thank you for all who have assembled in this place and pray that our being together will enhance each of our lives. Amen.

Source of all existence and Sustainer of all the worlds that are, make us aware that even though you are a High and Holy God you also are a God who is present within and among us. We are aware that you have called us to love you and one another, and we pray that you will remind us anew that love, to be love, must be expressed in action. Thus, may our being together inspire us to put our love into practice through lives of service to all whose lives touch ours. Amen.

All-encompassing God, whose we are and whose ways are to be reflected in every realm of life; grant that we will not think of you and be concerned to do your bidding only when we are in our houses of worship. Even as we meet as a civic body may we acknowledge that we are not the masters of our fates and the captains of our souls, that we are not owners but stewards of the gifts of life, and that we are the freest when we align our wills with yours. May this be reflected in what we do and say in the moments to come. Amen.

Prayers before Church Gatherings

Ever-beckoning God, who has called us into the church to accept the cost and joy of discipleship, we thank you for this local expression of the universal church. May we feel your presence within and among us as we meet on this occasion and deal with the agenda before us. May our deliberations and all of our decisions be acceptable to you, whom we seek to serve. Amen.

As we gather, gracious God, we pause to reflect on the importance of this church in our lives. For the opportunities of worship, education, service, and community it provides; for the support it offers in times of crisis and need; for the ties that bind our hearts in Christian love; we praise and thank you. May our lives be strengthened and enriched because we have been together in this time and place. We pray in the spirit of the one who is the Great Head of the church, Jesus, the Christ. Amen.

God of grace and God of glory, pour your power upon us who have accepted responsibilities in this church and who have gathered to discharge them. Grant us wisdom, grant us courage for the business of this hour and for the living of all of our days. May we ever hold before us the goals of your realm so that we will not fail others or you by what we do or fail to do. For we desire to serve you, whom we adore. Amen.

Ever-living God, who has given us the church for our instruction and inspiration, be with us as we seek to be faithful members of the body of Christ. Thank you, ever-giving God, for the gifts you have given us. May we use them in your service and to the end that your realm will come and your will be done on earth as it is in heaven. Amen.

God of Abraham and Sarah, God of Moses and Miriam, God of the prophets, and God of Jesus; we acknowledge that you are our God, too, and that we are your people. Individually, and corporately as this church, may we seek to fulfill what you require of us: to do justice, and to love kindness, and to walk humbly with you. Amen.

O God, who has called the worlds into being and created us in your image as persons who can love, feel, reason, and will: may we use each of these attributes as we share in the ministry of our church. May our labors build up this body which seeks to tell the story and carry on the ministry of Jesus, who was called "The One for Others" and in whose spirit and for whose sake we pray. Amen.

God of all goodness, faithful and changeless amid all of life's changes, our help and comfort when all else fails, and who promises to be present when even two or three have gathered in your name; bestow upon us your Spirit so that the words of our mouths, the meditations of our hearts, and the actions of our lives will be acceptable to you, our Rock and our Redeemer. Amen.

Invocations for Special Sundays

ADVENT

Eternal God, who has given us the church and its holy days for our preparation and inspiration; may these days of Advent help keep us focused on whose birthday we celebrate at Christmastime, the fact that our presence is more important than our presents, and that we can help bring peace and good will to all. Amen.

O God, for whose deliverance people had been praying for centuries, we pause in this Advent season to thank you for the enlightenment and answer to their prayers that came to our spiritual forebears in and through the life of Jesus. For he indeed revealed in his life and teachings your love and amazing grace, your will and ways, and showed humankind how to love you by loving others as well as ourselves. May the spirit of this Wonderful Counselor be evident in our lives during these days before Christmas. Amen.

Creator God, who comes to us again and again through the marvels of nature, in the person of Jesus, through the voice of conscience, and through your Spirit that dwells within us: make us receptive during these days of Advent to your still, small voice that calls us from childishness to childlikeness, from fear to faith, from greed to generosity, and from a life that is self-centered to one that is centered in you, the Ground of our Being. For we want our lives to reflect the spirit of the one whose birth soon will be celebrated! Amen.

Loving and faithful God, who loves us even when we are unloving and unlovable and who does not forsake us even when we turn our backs on you; we gather to worship and praise you for this Advent season. May the meaning and message of Christmas on which we focus in these days of preparation inspire us to be more loving and faithful both to you and others. Thank you, O God, for the birth and life of the one in whom we see your love and faithfulness incarnated, even Jesus, the Christ. Amen.

Ever-coming yet ever-present God, we gather to prepare ourselves for the celebration of Jesus' birth. For we need your help in preventing the pace, parties, and presents of this season from crowding out the true purpose of Christmas in our lives—the rebirth of the Christ's spirit which is hope, peace, and joy. Amen.

CHRISTMAS

Gracious and loving God, thank you for the gift of Christmas—the gift of your child Jesus who so enlightens us that we find in him the way, the truth, and the example of the life you would have us live. As we celebrate the anniversary of Jesus' birth into the world, may we invite your child to be born anew within us so that our lives will reflect the spirit of Christ and brighten the lives of all whose paths cross ours. Amen.

Creator God, in this Christmas season we pause to re-affirm that you have called us to give birth to the Babe of Bethlehem in our lives. We are to be the hands, the feet, the eyes, the ears, the mouth, the heart of Jesus in the world today. May this season inspire us to live in such a way that others will see the Christ in and through us. Amen.

As we gather to worship today, we thank you, O God, that Christmas need not be a once-a-year celebration. Grant that the loving, giving, sharing, and caring that were evident in our lives last week will continue to em-anate from us throughout the new year! Amen.

NEW YEAR'S

Holy One, whose presence we keenly feel during the Christmas season and whose child Jesus we especially are inspired to follow as we celebrate his birth; may we carry the spirit of Christmas with us into and throughout this new year. Make us wise enough to know that the feelings and actions of love, generosity, involvement, and compas-sion that have welled within us during the holidays are to be the hallmarks of our daily lives. To make them such is our New Year's resolution! Amen.

Ever-faithful, ever-loving God, who amid all the changes in life is always our Source of comfort, strength, and hope; we gather on this first Sunday of the new year to worship and praise your name. Forgive our failures of the past, and accept our gratitude for the gift of being able to begin again. Amen.

Eternal, always present God, on this first day of a new year we pause to thank you for your promise always to be with us. You have been our help in the past and are our hope for the year to come. Free us from the temptation to spend too much time regretting the past, and challenge us to face the future assured that you will give us the strength needed to face whatever comes our way. We pray in the spirit of the one whose birth we just celebrated, even Jesus, our Savior, who was called Emmanuel—"God with us." Amen.

Creator of Life, who ever was, is now, and ever shall be; God of change and God of new beginnings: we pause at the threshold of this new year to acknowledge that you were with us in the past and to affirm that you will be with us in the future. May our worship this day inspire us to make the most of and to put to the best use possible the new year that contains the future we will help to create. Amen.

Eternal God, as a new year begins, forgive our failures of the year now passed. Sustained by our faith that you are a loving and merciful God, may we go forward into the new year resolved better to keep your commandments, to be more appreciative of your blessings, and more closely to approximate the example for living found in the one whose birth we just celebrated, even Jesus, the Christ, in whose spirit we pray. Amen.

A WINTRY SUNDAY

O God, we come to worship this morning confessing that the weather just about has us down! This winter has been nearly too much for us. The snow, ice, and cold have caused us to be depressed, discouraged, discourteous, and short-tempered. We have found ourselves being crabby, unloving, and unlovable. We gather, therefore, recognizing our need for the warmth of your presence and the community and support of one another. May our lives be renewed by our worship, and may we find strength to meet the challenges of this new week. Amen.

LENT

We gather, O God, as pilgrims beginning our lenten journey. During this season may we seek to learn more truths about you, more clearly discern your will for our lives, and then more faithfully live in the loving and serving manner as did the Christ in whose spirit we pray. Amen.

Gracious God, in whose image we have been created—the image we see personified in Jesus, the Christ—in this season of Lent we come to rededicate ourselves to follow Jesus and to be willing to deny ourselves for the sake of others. Strengthen us to help bear the burdens of those less fortunate than we, for we know that when we love and serve them we love and serve you. We pray in the spirit and seek to follow the example of the one who came not to be ministered unto but to minister, even Jesus, the Christ. Amen.

PALM SUNDAY

Eternal God, today we join the crowds of every generation who, since the time of Jesus, have praised your name for his coming! For his entering Jerusalem in the spirit of peace, love, and servanthood, not as a militant conqueror, we give you thanks. May the example of Jesus lead us to relate to you and others in the same manner, not just today, but every day that the gift of life is ours! Amen.

Loving God, like the multitude surrounding Jesus on that first Palm Sunday, we often praise you with our lips but then reject you in our hearts. Forgive us for marching to the beat of drummers other than you. May we resolve today to get our lives back in step with your plan and purposes. Amen.

God of grace and God of glory, we praise you for Jesus, who rode into Jerusalem on a donkey's colt, victorious through love and not through power or violence. Help us to learn from his example that in living as servants and

seeking to meet others at their points of need, we find joy
and give you glory. Amen.

EASTER

O God, may we never forget the glory of Easter. To this
end, stamp indelibly in our lives the meaning and message
of this day: the assurance of your everlasting presence, the
ultimate triumph of goodness over evil, and our possibility of new beginnings! Amen.

We praise you, O God, for the glory of Easter and for
its message that day will succeed night, hope will van-
quish despair, peace will prevail over conflict, love will
conquer apathy and hatred, and life will outlast death!
May our lives be so filled with the Easter spirit that it
will shine through in what we say and do, just as
it shone through in the life of Jesus, the Christ. Amen.

O God, with the memories of another glorious Easter
still fresh in our minds, like the disciples of Jesus we
gather on this first day of the week to celebrate the experience of resurrection: the promise of hope in the midst of
despair, the possibility of new life before death, the assurance of continued life after death, and the reality of your
spirit that is always present within and around us. May
this and every Sunday be for us a "little Easter" that reminds us that Jesus is alive and that we are to be the
body of Christ in the world today. Amen.

FESTIVAL OF THE CHRISTIAN HOME

Creator God, who loves us as a father loves his daughter and who cares for us as a mother cares for her son, we gather to praise you for giving us life, to ask your forgiveness for the times when we do not use well the gift of life we have been given, and to resolve anew to be more the person you want us to be. Thank you for loving us even when we are unloving or feel that we are unlovable. We will try to do better! Amen.

O God, you are to us like an ideal mother and father. You love us "although" and not just "because"; you always are willing to listen; you always stand ready to help. Make us, we pray, better children of yours—willing to learn from you, concerned to be obedient to you, motivated to love you, and desirous of emulating you. Amen.

MEMORIAL DAY

Great and Gracious God, our help in ages past and our hope for years to come; we gather on this Memorial Day weekend to affirm, like Paul of old, that "whether we live or whether we die, we are God's." We pause to thank you for the lives and love of those who have died and who now live with you and also continue to live within us. For their memories that always will be ours, we praise you. Amen.

PENTECOST

Eternal God, on this day of Pentecost we remember and celebrate the birth of the Christian church. For those disciples of Jesus who resolved to be the ongoing body of Christ, for those of succeeding generations who have kept the church alive, for the many ways in which the church ministers to us today, we give you praise and thanks. Forgive us for taking the church for granted. And may our birthday gift to the church be a renewed commitment to be more faithful in our worship, our sharing, and our service. Amen.

As on that day of Pentecost long ago, so infuse us with your spirit, Holy One, that we might be overwhelmed by your presence within and among us! May we hear anew your call to be the body of Christ wherever we live or work or play, to the end that our daily lives will reflect the life and teachings of the one in whose spirit we pray. Amen.

FATHER'S DAY

We gather, O God, aware that today is designated as one on which to honor our fathers or their memories and also the attributes of fatherhood that we have learned from and experienced through Jesus, who called you Father. May our worship thus inspire us anew to exhibit these qualities by leading lives that are faithful, affectionate, thankful, honest, exemplary, and reverent. Amen.

God, our Creator, you are to us like a father. You love us no matter what; you are continually concerned for our welfare; you seek to influence and guide us in ways that will result in our betterment; you give us freedom to grow by making mistakes as well as by enjoying successes; you always stand ready to help and listen. Thank you, O God. May we be better, more appreciative, and more loving children. Amen.

FOURTH OF JULY

God of our forebears, and our God, too; we pause on this special day to offer thanks for the nation in which we live. We are grateful for those of the past whose ideals and actions gave birth to these United States. May our worship today remind us of our roots and motivate us to do whatever we can to help bring to fruition the vision of one nation, under you, where there is liberty and justice for all. Amen.

Creator God, who holds the whole world in your hands; we thank you this day for the part of your world called the United States of America. But may we never forget that we are part of a global village and that all people— red and yellow, black, brown, and white—are precious in your sight. Amen.

God of our mothers and fathers, we worship this day conscious of the heritage that is ours and mindful of those who conceived and gave birth to these United States. May our gratitude for their efforts and sacrifices be shown by our striving to keep burning brightly the torch they lit—a torch designed to reveal to all a nation whose sovereign is God, the One in whom we trust. Amen.

THANKSGIVING

Ever-present and ever-giving God, who has given us the gift of life and its attendant blessings, as we enter this week of Thanksgiving grant us one more gift—the gift of a grateful heart. Forgive us for taking life for granted and for complaining about what we lack instead of rejoicing over what we have. May our worship today enhance our gratitude! Amen.

We come to you, O God, as thankful people! We are mindful in this Thanksgiving season of our blessings, not just our difficulties; of our successes, not just our failures; of our assets, not just our liabilities; of our strengths, not just our weaknesses; of our joys, not just our sorrows. Grant us, we pray, the attitude of gratitude—not only in these coming days, but every day that life is ours. Amen.

Creating, ever-faithful, ever-giving, and ever-loving God, we gladly and gratefully gather to speak and sing your praise. On this Thanksgiving Sunday we are mindful of all that you have given us. We confess, however, that too often ours is only silent gratitude, which is of no use to you or to others. Thus we pray that we will be inspired anew intentionally and concretely to reflect and express our gratitude in what we say and in what we do, as did Jesus, the Christ, in whose spirit we pray. Amen.

Ever-giving and generous God, who loves us not because of our merits but just because we are; we pause in your presence, overwhelmed by our blessings. Life itself, family, friends, food, home, church, community, the marvels and beauty of creation, and other gifts too numerous to mention fill our lives to overflowing. Keep us, we pray, from ever taking for granted what we enjoy. And may we always remember that we are the caregivers and caretakers, not the owners, of all that seems to be ours. In gratitude and humility we pray. Amen.

CHRISTIAN EDUCATION

O God, Parent of Jesus the Great Teacher and our Parent; make us receptive to learning more about the one who is the Way, the Truth, and the Life. But as we learn, make us aware that we also teach by what we say and what we do. May our worship inspire us to be more receptive learners about and more faithful teachers of the Christian faith. Amen.

BIBLE PRESENTATION

Eternal God, whose Word is a lamp to our feet and a light to our paths, we thank you this day for the Bible that reveals your nature and teaches us how to live. We thank you, too, for the children who are the future of the church and the recipients of the heritage we are passing on. May our worship cause us to examine the example we set and motivate us to change if we might be causing little ones to stumble or err. Amen.

STEWARDSHIP

Gracious God, we gather for worship to be reminded of who and whose we are. You are our Creator; we are your daughters and sons. You have given us: the gift of life to enjoy but not to abuse; possessions to share but not to hoard; freedom to use with responsibility but not license; talents to use but not to allow to rust. So motivate us this day that we will more fully be the persons you want us to be. Amen.

Ever-giving God, who has revealed to us that it is more blessed to give than to receive and that when we lose our lives to your will and ways we, in truth, find ourselves; make us aware of how much you have given us. During these days when we are called to financial commitment, as we have freely received let us also freely give! Amen.

O God, whose child Jesus taught by the example of his life that it is better to give than to receive and to minister than to be ministered unto, inspire us to adopt a stance in life wherein we are concerned not so much with what we can get but with what we can give. For it is in giving that we receive; it is in serving that we find life that is abundant. Amen.

We pause, great and glorious God, to express our gratitude for all that we have been given by you and by those who have gone before us. Today we offer our special thanks for all of the churches of which we have been a part that have taught us about you, enriched our lives with countless friendships, served as channels for our outreach to others, and supported us in times of difficulty and sorrow. Inspire us, we pray, to keep this church alive and vital for your sake, for our sake, and for the sake of those who will come after us. We pray in the spirit of the one whose body we seek to be—Jesus, the Christ. Amen.

MUSIC RECOGNITION

God of harmony, who has put a song in our hearts, we have come this day to join the procession of those who have sung your praises throughout the centuries. For those who composed texts and music enabling them to be sung, we thank you. May their efforts refresh and renew us as we worship you in spirit and in truth. Amen.

Creator God, Orchestrator of the Universe; you desire to be the Conductor of our lives. Thus, we gather to worship to be reminded of the score you would have us follow and to rededicate ourselves to responding to your direction and living in harmony with one another. Amen.

NEW MEMBER RECEPTION

Gracious, glorious, and loving God, whom we have come to know, love, and serve because of the church that keeps alive the story of our faith, we rejoice today as we welcome new members into our community of faith. As they commit themselves to this local expression of your universal church, may we recommit ourselves to being faithful members who worship regularly, contribute generously, and share as able in the life and ministry of this congregation. Amen.

As we gather, loving and gracious God, we pause to reflect on the importance of this church in our lives. For the opportunities of worship, education, service, and community it provides; for the support it offers in times of crisis and need; for the ties, both old and new, that bind our hearts in Christian love; we praise and thank you. May our lives be strengthened and enriched because we have been together in this time and place. Then may we go forth to be the church wherever we are. We pray in the spirit of the one who is the Great Head of the church, Jesus, the Christ. Amen.

CHURCH ANNIVERSARY

We gather, eternal God, mindful of all that we enjoy because of the labors of others. The place where we sing your praises today was built by those who founded our church, and many of us "inherited" the chapel and sanctuary in which we regularly worship. May this service challenge us to consider what we will leave for those who will be a part of this church in the years to come. We pray in the spirit of the one who is the Cornerstone of the church, even Jesus, the Christ. Amen.

CHURCH CENTENNIAL

God of our forebears and our God as well, we thank you for the gift of this local expression of the church that for a century has told the story of Jesus and his love and has ministered in the name of Jesus to people within this church and beyond its walls. May we keep alive and pass on the heritage we have been given as we gather to worship, learn, enjoy community, and then go forth to serve you by serving others. Amen.

CONGREGATIONAL MEETING

We gather, O God, to reaffirm that we are the Body of Christ in this time and place, mindful that each of us members has duties to fulfill. Make us more keenly aware of our responsibilities to stay in close contact with the Body, to recognize the importance of every member, and to do whatever we can to build up this local expression of the Universal Church, whose cornerstone is the Christ. Amen.

Invocations for Any Sunday

Ever-present, ever-loving God, who seeks to mold us after your will so that we will bear the image of you, our Creator; may our worship today result in our being pliable people who, aware of our sin and shortcomings, rededicate ourselves to follow more closely the example for living found in Jesus, the Christ, in whose spirit we pray. Amen.

We have come to this place, O God, because it has been dedicated to your worship and because it is replete with reminders of you, the Holy One, who created us. We have come, not because we must but because we may; not out of fear but out of love; not to bask in our merits but to be buoyed by your acceptance, love, and mercy. Be within and among us, we pray, as we now worship you in spirit and in truth. Amen.

Holy God, Creator of all, whose will and ways we have found incarnated in the life of Jesus; keep us ever mindful that we are to follow the Christ but worship you. For it was to you, O God, that Jesus gave his allegiance as he grew in wisdom and stature and in favor with you and others. May this service inspire us to do the same. Amen.

Faithful God, our refuge and our strength, a very present help in trouble, our help in ages past and our hope for years to come; there are times in life when we need to be reminded that you never will forsake us and that you somehow will give us strength for the living of each day. May our worship this morning indelibly stamp these truths on our souls. Amen.

Nurturing God, Source of life, light, love, and truth; we approach you with expectancy and joy this day as we come to worship you. We know that as a parent loves a child, you love us. So may this hour motivate us to be childlike—loving, trusting, honest, and accepting—but not childish—self-centered, petulant, and immature. Amen.

God of the universe, Creator of all of earth's people: take away our myopia and remove our blinders as we worship you today. Improve our hearing so that we might hear the cries of your children who are less fortunate than we, and challenge us anew to respond to the words of your child Jesus, "As you did it to one of the least of these who are members of my family, you did it to me." Amen.

Creator and Creating God, who called the worlds into being and created us in your image; we confess that we often mistreat the world you have given us and forget that the setting for our span of life is your world, not ours. May our worship today motivate us to be better residents and caretakers of your earth and rivers and seas and sky. Amen.

Creator God, who has put a song in our hearts and who desires that we live in harmony with one another: may our worship gladden our spirits and motivate us to strive for a closer walk with you as we enter the path of this new week. Amen.

Compassionate Creator, who has given us voices with which to praise you, minds with which to seek you, hearts with which to love you, and lives with which to serve you, we gather this day to worship you in spirit and in truth. Renew us, refresh us, invigorate us, challenge us, inspire us, so that we may enter this new week assured of your love and comforted by the knowledge that your abiding presence within will enable us to face whatever comes our way in life. Amen.

Great, gracious, and gathering God, you have called us to be your people in this particular time and place. Thus, we have come to this house of worship desiring to see you more clearly, love you more dearly, and follow you more nearly. May we do so not just week by week, but day by day! Amen.

From our separate neighborhoods and communities we have gathered this day, O God, to affirm that no matter who we are or where we live or what our status of life, we are your children. Thank you for loving us and caring for and about us. Amen.

Caring Friend, whom we cannot love unless we love one another, and whom we cannot serve unless we serve one another; may our worship this day impress upon us that just as the cross is incomplete until the horizontal intersects the vertical, our relationship to you is incomplete until our lives meaningfully intersect the lives of those with whom we live and work and play and pray. Amen.

O God, Fountain of life, from whom flows more blessings than we can enumerate; we pause at the beginning of this new week to put ourselves in touch with you, the source of our spirits. Flood our lives with a sense of your presence, and keep us caught up in the current of your buoying love. Amen.

O God, you have been our help in ages past. But you want us to live in the present, and you are our hope for the future. Thank you for this day and for all of our tomorrows. For today is the first day of the rest of our lives. Amen.

Eternal God, you have called us into your church to be your people in this time and place. We have accepted your call, but often we forget our mission. Forgive us, renew us, and motivate us to go forth and be the church—active, functioning, contributing, loving members of the body of Christ whose lives make a difference! Amen.

Creator God, who desires for us wholeness and health, we open our lives to your spirit. Come in, and refresh us, renew us, restore us. May our worship remind us that the gifts of your abiding presence, your continual love, and your sustaining strength enable us to face every day of our lives, no matter what they may bring. For this we praise and thank you. Amen.

O God, we have come to this sanctuary, not just to be observers or to be entertained, but to join others in worshiping you. So open our minds and spirits that we might be aware of your presence in our midst. In this hour may we reflect on your power and goodness, seek forgiveness for our failures and wrongdoing, discern how we should live, and renew our commitment to follow you. Then may we go forth to love and serve you by loving and serving one another. Amen.

For voices with which to praise you, for hands with which to serve you, for minds with which to know you, and for hearts with which to love you, we thank you, O God. May our worship this day inspire us to a higher plane of living so that we will become more fully the persons you want us to be. Amen.

Good, great, and gracious God, who rejoices with us in our times of joy and is our refuge and strength in times of trouble, we have come to worship you in spirit and in truth and to reflect on your purposes for our lives. May the hymns we sing and the music and words we hear inspire and challenge us more closely to approximate the life of Jesus, in whose spirit we pray. Amen.

We gather, O God, to worship and praise you for all that you have given us. You love us just because we are, not because of who we are. You have blessed us because you are gracious, not because we have earned your grace. May this hour spent with you and one another motivate us to be more fully the people you intend and want us to be. Amen.

Caring Creator, ever within as well as around us, our Constant Companion as we traverse the hills and valleys of life; we gather in this place seeking to reestablish conscious contact with you, the Ground of our Being. Melt us, mold us, fill us, use us—for your sake, for the Christ's sake, and for the sake of others. For it is in loving that we are loved, in giving that we receive, and in serving that we are served. Amen.

God of Abraham, Sarah, Moses, and Jesus, and our God, too; we join the procession of those who down through the ages have sought to serve and love you with heart, soul, mind, and strength. We thank you this day for your ancient but timeless laws that offer guidelines for our daily living. Forgive us for the times we have disregarded them, and may we do a better job of following you day by day. Amen.

Caring Creator and Persuasive Presence, whose love surrounds us, whose strength supports us, whose truth enlightens us, and whose spirit guides us; you have given us a pattern for daily living in Jesus, the Christ. For his life and teachings, for showing us the way, and for the revelation that you are always with us, we offer our heartfelt thanks. Forgive us for the times when we have turned our backs on the example of Jesus, and make us more like the one in whose spirit we pray. Amen.

We have come to your house, O God, to worship and sing your praise. For you are the loving source of our lives who calls us to love you by serving others. And your indwelling spirit strengthens and enables us to face this new day and week in the hope and assurance that you will enable us to face and contend with whatever comes our way. For being our Creator and Sustainer, thank you! Amen.

Ever-present God, who always is within and around us and who gives us courage for the living of each day; we gather to praise you for guiding and upholding our lives. Make us more keenly aware of your still, small voice that calls us to be the best that we can be and that reminds us that we never walk alone! Amen.

Loving and merciful God, who has called us to be your servants in the service of others and who has given us talents enabling us to serve; forgive us for those times when we have buried our gifts and thus failed to be there for others and to do what we could have done to make ours a better world in which to live. May our worship today inspire us to say, "Here am I, God," and then to go forth to live in the manner of the Christ, whose name we profess. Amen.

Sovereign God, vaster than our minds can fathom yet as intimate as love itself, we gather to profess that you are our God and we are your people. Forgive us for at times forgetting whose we are and thereby denying the relevance of your will and ways. Claiming your forgiving grace, we rededicate ourselves to following more faithfully and fully the life and teachings of Jesus, the Christ, in whom we see you most clearly and completely revealed. Amen.

Eternal God, who loves each of us as a parent loves a child, we pause to remember your amazing grace and your perennial and protective presence. You indeed are our refuge and strength and present with us both in good and in difficult times. Because you love us and always are with us, in gratitude we rededicate ourselves to following

Jesus' commandment to love you with heart, soul, mind, and strength, and our neighbors as ourselves. Amen.

Loving, living God, we have come to this place dedicated to your worship because we seek to have our lives refreshed and renewed. Sometimes we need to be reminded that we are to do what is right, that we are to speak the truth from our hearts in love, that the words we say are not to hurt or slander, and that we are to do no evil to others. Forgive us for the times when we have failed to live in this manner in the past week, and enable us to do a better job of living and loving in this new week that lies ahead. Amen.

Ever-present Source of life and strength, we pause now to become aware of your spirit that always is around and within us, just waiting to be recognized and affirmed. Forgive us for not accepting your power when we are powerless and your assistance when we fall or fail. May this hour with you and your people refresh and renew us so we better can live each day that is ours. Amen.

Holy, gracious, and everlasting God, we gather to sing and speak your praise. You love us as a parent loves a child. When we are weak you offer us your strength. When we are brokenhearted you offer us your comfort and healing. When we stumble or fall you offer to help us. When we sin you offer us your forgiveness. For being our help in the past and our hope for the future, we offer you our thanks. Amen.

You have called us, O God, to worship you in spirit and in truth, and we have gathered for this purpose. Open our eyes to the beauty of the world you have created; open our ears to your still, small voice that seeks to influence us; open our hearts to your amazing grace and forgiving love. Being thus reminded of your greatness, your guidance, and your goodness, may we seek to live as did Jesus, the Christ, in whose spirit we pray. Amen.

O God, who comes to us as Creator, Refuge, and Fortress, we remember you this day as Shepherd—one who cares about who we are, where we are, and how we are doing. You are our Shepherd who knows our joys and our sorrows, our gifts, and our needs. Lead and guide us this day and throughout this new week. As sheep follow their shepherd, may we follow you, as did Jesus, the Christ, who also was like a shepherd and called people to follow him. Amen.

Creator and loving God, who desires to turn our weeping into joy and our mourning into dancing, who stays with us during the dark nights of our souls until we experience the light of life once again; we give you thanks for your constant love and powerful presence. May our worship today remind us of our call to follow you by showing love to you and others, as did Jesus, the Christ, in whose spirit we pray. Amen.

Creator God, Fountain of Life, whose constant presence, amazing grace, and law of love nurture and sustain us each day; we have come to recommit ourselves to you. For in and through you is life that is both abundant and eternal. You have called us to be your people; so we respond by asking you to melt us, mold us, fill us, use us, so that our lives will more closely approximate the life of Jesus, the Christ, whose we are and whom we seek to serve. Amen.

Eternal, ever-present God, we pause in your presence to thank you for being within and around us throughout life. When we are weak, you are to us like a rock. When we are buffeted or endangered by life's events, you are our fortress. For hearing us, for delivering and saving us, we are forever grateful and therefore have come to praise and honor you, as did Jesus, in whose spirit we pray. Amen.

Prayers for Special Sundays

ADVENT

O God, Christmas will be here in __ days. This morning help us face the question of whether or not we will be ready for Christmas. But help us consider the question not from the perspective of will our presents be purchased, our cards and packages be mailed, our baking done. Rather, will we really be prepared? Will we have rethought the deeper meaning of Christmas? Will it dawn on us anew that Christmas means that you are always with us; that in Jesus we find the human example of how we are meant to live; that the greatest gifts we can give and receive are love, joy, peace, and hope?

Only __ more days. But thank you, God, that we don't have to wait. We can begin living Christmas right now! Amen.

Creator God, Source of all that we have and are, Sovereign of peace, Strength of our lives, Sustainer of the universe: in the humility of the shepherds and the expectancy of the Magi we prayerfully pause in your presence.

We humbly bow before you because we recognize that life and light and love came down in a special way at Christmas. We are reminded during these December days that in the one who was born in Bethlehem we see human life as it is meant to be lived; we find light that pierces the gloom and enables us to cope with and overcome even

the most difficult circumstances that come our way; and
we are reminded that no matter who or what we are we
are lovable and loved by you, our Creator, and thus we
can love ourselves and others.

And, Great and Gracious God, we are expectant today because we are aware that Christmas brings out the
best in ourselves and in others. We know that we enjoy
life much more when we and others are more concerned
to: give than to receive, forgive than to harbor grudges,
love than to be indifferent, cheer than to chastise.

We pray that Christmas for us will be not just a day
but a spirit that we will keep alive throughout the year
because we continually invite the Babe of Bethlehem to be
born anew in and then to be expressed through our lives.
Amen.

Great, gracious, and giving God, whose gift of Jesus we
celebrate during this season as we prepare for the anniversary of his birth; as the shepherds and Magi left their
fields and homes to worship the Christ child, so we have
come to this sanctuary to worship you.

We praise and thank you this day, O God, for the
revelation of your will and ways for our lives that was
bundled in the Babe of Bethlehem. For as he grew in wisdom and stature and in favor with you and others, people
ever since have witnessed the incarnation of how you
want us to live. How grateful we are for the human example of one: who loved you and himself enough so that
he could love even those whom he did not like, who re-
sisted the temptations that he experienced, who shared

his deepest feelings and desires with you in prayer, who
enjoyed the company of others because he knew that
alone he was incomplete, who forgave those who
wronged him, who found meaning and purpose in life
by being there for others.

Forgive us for the times and ways in which, during
the past week, we failed to emulate the example of Jesus.
Strengthen us and renew our resolve in the days to come
to give birth to Jesus' spirit, to be the hands and feet and
mouth and heart—the body of Christ—as in gratitude we
offer you, O God, the gift of our lives. Amen.

CHRISTMAS EVE

Creating, loving, holy God, your Spirit, will, and ways
clearly and unforgettably were revealed in the life and
teachings of the one whose birth we celebrate within the
hour. We pause, therefore, bathed in the light of the
Christmas star, to examine whether or not our lives sil-
houette your image in which we have been created.

This evening we would unwrap the baby Jesus from
his swaddling cloths and let him grow into the one who
became the Christ and our Redeemer. Thus on this
Christmas Even we ask some Christmas questions. Jesus
saw the good and the potential in others. Do we? Jesus
knew that it is when we give that we receive. Do we?
Jesus helped people just because they were human beings,
not because of who or what they were. Do we? Jesus
knew whose he was and thus sought to show his love
and devotion to you by loving you with heart, soul, mind,
and strength, and his neighbor as himself. Do we?

May we truly celebrate Christmas tomorrow and then keep alive the spirit of Christmas by daily emulating the one whose name we bear and in whose spirit we pray—the Babe of Bethlehem who became the Savior of us all. Amen.

How easy it is to pray tonight, O God. This season, and Christmas Eve especially, makes us feel unusually close to you and to one another. Perhaps it is because Christmas heightens in us those feelings that are so in harmony with your spirit: love, compassion, joy, gratitude, expectancy, hope.

Whatever the case, we are experiencing the warmth of your and others' love; we feel motivated by your compassion to love and give of ourselves; in spite of whatever might cause us despair, there is within us an unquenchable joy; we are overwhelmed with gratitude for all that we have; we find ourselves facing confidently the future; we are engulfed by a hope that assures us that your strength will enable us to face all of our todays and tomorrows.

Keep these many manifestations of your spirit, the Christmas Spirit, burning brightly within us each day we live. And keep us ever sensitive to how and with whom we can share the light that comes from the recognition of your presence and the desire to do your will—the light that was kindled most brightly in the one who was born the Babe of Bethlehem and who became your child, our Sovereign, our Savior, and the Light of the world—even Jesus, the Christ, in whose spirit we pray. Amen.

CHRISTMAS

O God of Christmas and of every day, God of Jesus, and our God, too; how rare the opportunity for us to join in worship on the anniversary of the birth into the world of your child, who ever since has embodied for us a new and heightened expression of your presence and your love.

We thank you for this day for which we have been preparing for weeks. For this is the day that especially reminds us of the importance of caring, hoping, repenting, intending, sharing, thanking, meditating, adoring, and serving.

Forgive us for the occasions when these traits have been absent in our relating to you and/or others. May we keep alive within us these manifestations of the Christmas spirit not only today but in all of our tomorrows. Amen.

NEW YEAR'S

O God, whose commandments we would keep, whose community we would enjoy, and to whose service we would be loyal, we pause before you as we cross the threshold of another year. For its open doors of possibilities and its hope of new beginnings, we give you thanks.

We are especially grateful that at the core of our faith is the message that life is a matter of becoming and that we can begin again. We confess that there is some of the year just passed that we would like to forget and erase: words that hurt rather than helped, acts that we know were sinful. Some of these blots and stains we can remove by corrective action in the days to come, and we pray from you the desire and strength to right these wrongs. But some of our mistakes are irreparable, and all we can do is sincerely to ask your forgiveness while at the same time vowing not to repeat our errors of the past.

So thank you for the new page in our lives. May the entries we make on it be in harmony with your design for us. And months from now may we be more satisfied with this year's page than last year's. For it is a reasonable expectation that we should be better and worthier at the end of the year than we are at the beginning! May this be our goal. Amen.

MARTIN LUTHER KING JR. DAY

God of the universe and of all people, Parent of the human family in which we are sisters and brothers of one another, we pause to offer our special prayers prior to a significant national holiday.

You have called us, O God, to be dreamers of dreams and to dream that one day ours indeed will be one nation, under you, with liberty and justice for all. We confess, however, that we dream too much and act too little. We are not always color blind. We accept and judge others on the basis of how they are different from us, thus erecting barriers because of race, class, creed, or sexual orientation. We forget that red or yellow, black or white, all are precious in your sight.

Thank you, God, for people like Martin Luther King Jr.—those who in the past and even today challenge us to ensure that none will be denied life, liberty, or the pursuit of happiness; none will be denied justice or opportunities. For all of us are persons, not pigmentations! Amen.

Super Bowl Sunday

God of grace and God of glory; Fountain of light and truth; Lover of every soul; Source of all that we have and are; Sustainer of our lives: we have gathered for worship on a super day as well as Super Sunday.

We confess, Holy One, that often we become confused about what is important in life and that our priorities are all mixed up. There are times when we feel that football is as important as faith, when games are of more interest that grace, when huddles attract our attention more than homelessness, when plays have more stature than prayer, when coaches seem on a par with the Christ, when success can be substituted for sportsmanship, when salaries make us forget about stewardship, when touchdowns are equated with theology.

Restore us to our senses, O God. Let us remember that persons are more important than points, that serving is more important than Super Bowls, that worship is more important than winning, and that the love we experience coming from you and one another enables us to get through the periodic losses that come our way in life. Amen.

Abraham Lincoln's Birthday

Gracious and glorious God, whose principles for living have been exemplified by a great cloud of witnesses who

have gone before us, this morning we are especially reminded of the historic hero whose birth is remembered
this weekend. From the life of this man who became Pres-
ident of our nation and preserver of the Union we can
learn so many lessons: the value of working diligently to
achieve our goals, the need to try again when we fail, the
strength that comes from hope, the immorality of dis-
criminating against another person because of the color
of his skin or her station in life.

As Abraham Lincoln was called the Great Emancipator, help us not to forget that you, O God, are the greatest
emancipator. For when we earnestly seek to follow your
intention for us, when we consciously attempt to model
our lives after that of Jesus: we are set free from the
bondage of sin; we are saved from an existence that has
little or no meaning to a life that has purpose and direction; we are delivered from fear and filled with hope; we
are given the grace to forget the past, begin again, and
keep on becoming.

Thank you for standing ready to help us be freed to
become more fully human and to actualize more completely the love, compassion, and penchant for serving
you and others that wells within us but whose floodgates
we need to open wider. May the realization of more of
our potential be our goal today and every day that we are
privileged to live. Amen.

VALENTINE'S DAY

God of Love, whose love best was illustrated long ago
in the way Jesus of Nazareth loved you and those with

whom he shared life, we pause in your loving presence to reaffirm that you are our God and we are your people, to be reminded that you are like an ideal loving parent, and to reassess our lives in the light of your love.

Thank you for loving and caring for and about us. Forgive us for the times when we have failed to love you and others as we know we should. We confess that too often we take you for granted and forget that there are some rules and regulations by which you would have us live; too often we think that if we do not like someone we are excused from loving that person; too often we view others as objects and not persons, thus demeaning and dehumanizing them.

O God, on this day associated with love, make us better lovers of you and one another. Help us to notice, help us to care, help us to be available to any person in need. For in loving others we love you, in serving others we serve you, in ministering to others we find our lives strengthened and enriched. Amen.

LENT

Great, gracious, and giving God; Confidant of the confessing, Healer of the hurting, Help of the helpless, Hope of the hopeless, Light of the lost, Lover of the loveless, Savior of the sorrowing; when we pause long enough to consider who you are and how you have enriched and undergirded our lives, we are humbled by the realization of how great you are and how amazing is your grace!

Yet, in spite of your goodness to us, we too often take you for granted and admit you only to the periphery of our lives. We think of you periodically; we follow you half-heartedly and haphazardly; we love you luke-warmly.

Faithful Father, Marvelous Mother, Pardoning Parent; our prayer this morning is that we will be more intentional about our Christian living. May the season of Lent that we enter this week be a time when we more consciously practice your presence—asking ourselves: What would Jesus do in this situation? How would he relate to this person or that?"

May we be more faithful followers of the one whose name we profess, ones who practice what we believe and preach, and among those who show others, not tell them, the way! Amen.

Living God of all who live, for whose spirit we long, to whose voice we would listen, and from whom we would learn; we pause in your presence in this Lenten season.

Educate, empower, encourage, energize, and enlighten us as we embark on our journey designed to enable us more efficaciously to emulate the empathetic example of Jesus.

Nudge us so that we will not be so nonchalant about these noteworthy days. May we never neglect our need for nurturing so we can be more than nominal disciples.

Transform our tendency to thirst for the trite and trivial. Turn our thoughts, O Transcendent One, toward trying to temper our lives with the timeless traits of tenderness, thankfulness, thoughtfulness, and truthfulness.

Creator God, we love you; we embrace you; we need you; we trust you. Amen.

Creative and Creating God, whose artistry that blanketed the earth with snow this past week is symbolic of the way in which your love blankets our lives, we come to offer our lives in worship—-not because we must but because we may, not because we have earned your love but because you love us just because we are, not because we seek to be exceptions to the human race but because we seek strength for facing the difficulties that are a part of being human.

As we thank you for your love and presence within and around us, we confess that sometimes we have been unloving toward and not present for others. For being apathetic rather than active, critical rather than caring, disdainful rather than devoted, griping rather than grateful, petulant rather than peaceful, neglectful rather than nurturing, spiteful rather than supportive, thoughtless rather than thoughtful, forgive us.

As we move toward the conclusion of Lent and anticipate the celebration of Easter, may Easter's message of the hope of new life before death become a reality as we strive to live our lives as Jesus lived—as your children who, knowing that we are loved, love you, ourselves, and others. Amen.

God of winter and God of springtime, who created the universe with its changing seasons, we in your church thank you for the season of Lent. For in these days we have been learning more about how you want us to live by reflecting on the life and teachings of Jesus.

Today we especially thank you for his life. For here was a human being like us who was so sensitive to your will and who so used his potential that he became the example of full humanity. Jesus learned and practiced the truths: that in your will is true peace, that your strength enables us to cope with life, that good can come from evil and tragedy, that there is hope in the midst of despair, that love is the most powerful force in the world.

As Jesus matured and grew in his relationship with you to the point where these truths became part and parcel of his daily living, may we similarly hunger and thirst for this goal. For you have created us for yourself, and we are restless and unfulfilled until we are consciously committed to you. Amen.

ONE GREAT HOUR OF SHARING

God of grace and God of glory; God of winter and God of springtime; God of the past, the present, and the future; God of North America, South America, and every continent; God of outer space and the inner spaces of our lives; we pause to acknowledge that you are our Creator and that there is within us a God-shaped vacuum that when left unfilled results in our lives being shallow and without direction. We confess that too often your rightful place is filled with trivia, and we push your will and ways to the periphery of our lives. We call upon you only when convenient or when emergencies arise. Forgive us for being only sporadically faithful.

During these coming lenten days when we will be challenged to consider what we will give to One Great Hour of Sharing next Sunday, make us aware of how much we have in comparison to the vast majority of the world's population. We do not go hungry as do people in Africa. We are not homeless as are people who live even in our own communities. We are not confined to dilapidated, crime-filled housing projects as are many who live within a few miles of us but who, since out of our sight, rarely are thought of by us who live amid beautiful surroundings.

Loving God, confront us with the truth that how much we care is reflected in how much we share. Since we have been so richly blessed, may we be more concerned to be givers, not takers. For we seek to be more dedicated disciples of the one whose life reflected that it is in giving that we receive, it is in losing our lives that we find and save them—Jesus, the Christ, in whose spirit we pray. Amen.

EASTER

Ever-beckoning God, you continually call us from: apathy to action, callousness to caring, faithlessness to faithfulness, greed to generosity, haughtiness to humility, hopelessness to hope, meaninglessness to meaning, sadness to solace, sin to servanthood—in other words, from life to death. Forgive us for so often not heeding your call and remaining in the ruts that sink life below what it might and can be.

Thank you for Easter. For its message is that we can grow and change; we can rise to higher planes of personal living; there is hope in the midst of our despair; there is joy in spite of sadness.

As Jesus' tomb stood open on that first Easter morning, on this Easter may our lives stand open to your spirit that can breathe into us newness of life. Fill us with the radiance of this day so that your love may stream in and through us, bringing light and life to a world that often walks in shadows and death. Amen.

Eternal, ever-loving, ever-present God of Easter and our everyday existence:

Accept our accolades and ascriptions of awe and adoration as we assemble in this sanctuary today.

Save us from a saccharine, sanctimonious, social celebration of what should be a saving, spiritual, and symbolic Sunday and season.

Thank your for Easter's teaching and truth that temptations, testings, troubles, trials, and tragedy can be transformed into triumph.

Enable, energize, and empower us to the end that the evidences of Easter will be embodied and exemplified in our lives.

Reawaken, renew, and redirect us so that we might rededicate ourselves to realizing the resurrection that reposes in our lives and desires release. Amen.

EARTH DAY

Creating God, Creator of the planets, the sun, the moon, the stars, and of life itself; we, the epitome of your creation, pause to worship you with words and songs of praise! You are our God; we are your people; and we have come to affirm this fact!

Yet, Eternal Spirit, we confess that we do not always live as though we are yours. You created us to care for one another and the world in which we live. Too often, however, we uncaringly treat others as things to be used, and we thoughtlessly abuse the world into which we were born. Forgive us, we pray.

Thank you, God, for Earth Day and for its reminders and challenge for each of us to be better caretakers of the planet you have entrusted to us. Inspire us this day to be better citizens of this earth: who seek to conserve and not waste exhaustible natural resources, who do not spoil the beauties of nature by littering or trashing, who urge our elected officials to curtail deforestation and pollution.

May we go forth from this place with the words of Edward Everett Hale ringing in our ears and informing our lives: "I am only one, but still I am one. I cannot do everything, but still I can do something; and because I cannot do everything I will not refuse to do the something that I can do." Amen.

Gracious God of the universe, who has the whole world in your hands, we, your children, the highest form of your creation, pause in your presence to share with you our deepest feelings in this time of prayer. There is so much going on around us, and as we pause to sort out the world in which we live we realize that there is much that we need to appropriate into our lives.

Earth Day has come and gone. But, Creator God, keep us ever aware that you have entrusted to us the care of our planet Earth. You have given it to us to use but not to abuse. Our world has natural resources that we are to conserve for the world of our children and our children's children, resources that we are not to deplete just for the sake of our own pleasure or comfort. Thus, make us so responsive to conservation and recycling that every day will for us, in a sense, be Earth Day.

We live in a day and age when Hollywood and television seem to create for our nation's children, and sometimes for us, our heroic figures and role models. Thus, O God of love, may Teenage Mutant Ninja Turtles and Power Rangers, with their penchant to use force and violence, not become characters whom we seek to honor or emulate.

And, O Holy One, who continually beckons and who always responds to the invitation to enter our lives, make us as desirous to find your will for our lives and the insights provided for our daily living that are to be found in the Bible as we are concerned to find Waldo in the pages of the books where he is hidden.

Finally, O God, our help in ages past and our hope for years to come, hear the silent prayers we offer for persons who are especially near and dear to us and for situations in which we have a particular interest. Amen.

DAYLIGHT SAVINGS TIME

God of the past and future, God of the changing seasons; we have gathered in this place dedicated to your worship after a night made shorter because one hour passed in an instant. That hour, O God, is gone and cannot be recovered.

We did not have an opportunity to use wisely or to waste that hour. But, O Source of life, there are so many other hours that are at our disposal. We thank you for them, and we also ask your forgiveness for those hours that we have used and continue to use unwisely.

We confess, Pardoning Parent, that we waste so many of our hourly gifts: by looking for faults in other people; by holding on to grudges; by postponing those good deeds that we think about doing, with the result that they remain only good intentions; by being so consumed with our work that we neglect our families, friends, and faith; by spinning our wheels rather than making a decision and moving on with our lives.

Enable us, we pray, to make better use of our gift of life's hours: by taking time to observe the beauty of the earth in springtime; by being alert to and responding to the needs of others, including our family members; by spending some time each day in meditation, reflection, and prayer; by giving back to you at least one hour each week in which we join others in offering you our praise and thanks; by doing at least one thing each week that will make our world a better place in which to live.

Thank you, God, for this and every hour of our lives! Amen.

FESTIVAL OF THE CHRISTIAN HOME

O God, whose children we are and who is like a parent to us, we have come to worship you on this special day that reminds us of the importance of the families of which we have been and are now a part.

Many of us have so much for which to be grateful. For parents who gave us birth and nurtured us with love; for sisters and brothers with whom we have shared many experiences; for a husband or wife whose very life gives meaning, purpose, and fulfillment to our own; for sons and daughters whom we love and in whom we have invested ourselves; thank you!

Heavenly Parent, help us realize how much poorer we would be without these relationships. Therefore, may we not take them for granted but do all within our power to strengthen, enrich, and preserve them. Amen.

MEMORIAL SUNDAY

God of us who are living and those who have preceded us in death, you whose we are whether we live or die, our hearts are overflowing with the gift of remembrance as we worship you this day. How great and humbling is our debt to the past and to those present with us now only in our memories. For the lives of those to whom this day we dedicate lasting memorials that will enhance the ministry of our church and for others near and dear to us who now from their labors rest, we give you thanks. For those who throughout the history of our nation have given their lives in behalf of freedom, justice, and peace, we express to you our gratitude.

Guide and sustain us, O God, as we receive their inheritance, defend it, invest it, and share it with the world. Keep us faithful to the qualities of personhood and nationhood that are acceptable to you so that we, too, may leave for others a heritage that is imperishable and undefiled. Amen.

CONFIRMATION

Creating and loving God, we pause in your presence on this day of Confirmation—the day when __ of your children make promises to enter into a covenant with you and this church.

Our prayer this day is one of gratitude and petition. We offer our thanks for these young people soon to be confirmed and for their families. We thank you for the time and energy these youths have invested to prepare themselves for this hour when they consciously and publicly accept the Christian faith as their way of life and when they become official members of the church—the body that seeks to carry on the mission and ministry of Jesus, the Christ.

We pray that they will take seriously the commitment they make this morning and that their families and we their friends will offer our support and encouragement to the end that they will feel this to be a day of spiritual significance and not simply the fulfillment of a social custom. May these confirmands not forget, but be faithful to, their confirmation vows.

But, O God, our prayer also is one of confession. We who are members of your church confess that we often forget or take lightly the vows we took and the promises made when we embraced the Christian faith and became a part of a local expression of the body of Christ. The activities of our daily living and our being faithful members of the church often have been less than exemplary. Forgive us, and as once again we hear promises made and vows accepted, may we reaffirm them in our hearts and rededicate ourselves to being more faithful and effective witnesses of your presence and love in our world. Amen.

FATHER'S DAY

O God, on this particular day, to call you Father has special significance. For today we pay tribute to our fathers or their memories, and we are especially mindful of the attributes of fatherhood. Yes, many of us are thinking with gratitude of that man who has or had such great influence on his or her life, that man who seeks or sought to embody the ideals of fatherhood.

For what is a father? A father is: fair, faithful, and forgiving; able, accepting, and authentic; temperate, thankful, and thoughtful; honest, honorable, and hospitable; embracing, empathetic, and exemplary; reasonable, receptive, and responsive.

As we thank you for these qualities in our father, we are grateful that they are your attributes, too. And, O God, we pray that these same traits also might be evident in our lives. Amen.

FOURTH OF JULY

God of all the nations, Parent of all humankind, Good Shepherd of all who will follow you; as we approach the anniversary of the birth of our nation we are mindful of the heritage we enjoy as citizens of these United States of America. For those who created a new republic sought to base it upon the foundation of noble ideals. They affirmed that you are the Supreme Judge of the world. They affirmed that all people are created with equal and inalienable rights, including life, liberty, and the pursuit of happiness.

We confess, however, that all too often we have forgotten or forsaken the heritage entrusted to us by our founding fathers and mothers. Instead of making you our Supreme Judge we have followed the dictates of our own consciences, even when they conflicted with your divine will. Our guidelines more and more have become "Is it good for the economy?" or "Is everyone else doing it?" rather than "Is it right or wrong?" And instead of recognizing all people as your children and that we are all brothers and sisters, we have discriminated against and put down those who differ from us in color of skin, or in sexual orientation, or in religious faith, or in economic status.

Forgive us. And as we celebrate the birth of our nation may each of us resolve to do a better job of making ours one nation under you, with liberty and justice for all. Amen.

Wise and wonderful God, Creator of the universe and ultimate source of life's blessings, we pause in awe and humility as we ponder your greatness and your goodness. We are amazed at the world in which we live, with all of its natural resources and its natural laws that have brought order out of chaos. We are humbled by the miracle of birth and life, for they remind us that there is a power greater than we.

As we approach another anniversary of the birth of our nation, we give you thanks for the heritage that is ours. For the Native Americans who saw you in the forces of nature—sun, moon, stars, clouds, rain—and who sought to conserve the land and animal life, we thank you. For the Pilgrims who uprooted themselves from their homeland and came to these shores so they could be free to worship in ways meaningful to them, we thank you. For the founders of our nation who affirmed "In God we trust," we thank you.

This morning we ask you to forgive us for not taking better care of those who were here before the colonists arrived and for too often despoiling the beauty and wasting the exhaustible resources of land and animal life. Forgive us, too, for taking for granted our freedom to worship, that too often results in our neglecting this facet of life. And forgive us for putting our trust in the many gods that sometimes crowd you off center stage—the stock market, the games we play, our penchant to please ourselves instead of you.

As the Fourth of July dawns, may it dawn upon us that from time to time we need to examine our heritage and do a better job of caring for others, caring for our God-given resources, and caring about you! Amen.

LABOR DAY

Creator God, the Labor Day weekend is a fascinating one! It reminds us of the work we are privileged to do and by which we earn our daily bread. It provides a holiday on which we can relax from our usual labor and play. It contains this Sunday when we can come to your house to spend an hour worshiping you.

This morning, however, we confess that our lives are not as integrated and whole as we would like them; our relationships are not as meaningful and satisfying as we desire. Help us to understand that this is because we are confused about the roles of work, play, and worship in our lives. For we tend to worship our work, to work at our play, and to play at our worship.

Forgive us. And may this special time in your presence start us on the road toward the goal of our work being a means and not an end, our play being fun, and our worship being real. Amen.

BEGINNING OF THE FALL SEASON

O God, in your Word we read that for everything there is a season. The summer has been a time for us to change the rhythm of our existence. Less structured schedules have permitted us to alter the pattern woven by our lives.

But now that fall fast approaches we find our pace

quickening. Activities that demand our time and attention are resuming; the days seem to pass more swiftly.

As we readjust our inner and outer timetables, motivate us to give your church high priority in our lives. For we need the opportunities it provides for worship, study, support, and community. But the church also needs us to carry on its ministries by investing our time, our abilities, and our resources in its mission.

So bless us as a congregation as we begin a new program year. May we be a church and not a club, pioneers and not just settlers, an outpost as well as a sanctuary! Amen.

CHRISTIAN ENLISTMENT

Creator God, from whom springs life itself, give us this day grateful hearts for all of the blessings that have been ours in the past, that we enjoy even today, and that we know will come our way in the future.

As we count our blessings, may we not overlook this church of which we are a part. For its being here to minister to us at birth, at baptism, at confirmation, at marriage, at death; for its teaching our children and youth and us adults more about your Word and way of life; for its worship that enriches and inspires our lives; for its being a channel through which we can serve and help others both near and far away; for the community and joy of human relationships it makes possible; for the counsel and support it offers during times of personal confusion or trauma; we thank you.

But may our gratitude be deeper than mere lip service. And because a measure of the importance we attach to various facets of life is the monetary investment we are willing to make in them, stir and move us during these days of stewardship commitment to offer more than just a token or the left-overs. Amen.

THANKSGIVING

Ever-loving God of grace and God of glory, who empowers us for the living of our days, we gather in this place dedicated to your worship and service as we enter this week of Thanksgiving. We are grateful for this special season that reminds us of blessings that we sometimes take for granted. Thus, today accept our gratitude for the gifts of: thinking, hugs, acceptance, nature, kindnesses, salvation, goals, identity, vocation, ideals, nation, guidance.

Forgive us for sometimes forgetting or using unwisely these gifts that are ours. And may we be motivated to express our gratitude for your innumerable gifts by seeking to live as you would have us live—by loving you with heart, soul, mind, and strength, and our neighbor as ourselves. We pray in the spirit of another of your gifts to us, Jesus, the Christ, in whom we have seen the way, the truth, and the life. Amen.

CHURCH ANNIVERSARY

Eternal God of the past, the present, and the future, today we are especially mindful of each of these dimensions of life.

The past seems but as yesterday as we recall the history of your local church called _____: how it began as a dream in the minds of a few and was transformed into a reality that has profoundly influenced and effected the lives of us assembled here and others. For the personal commitment and the stewardship of time, energy, talents, and resources of all who have shared in its life, we give you thanks. We thank you, too, for the memories of people and events connected with the past __ years—many joyful, some sad—but all of which are woven into the tapestry of our lives and thus have helped make us who and what we are today.

And yes, we thank you for today: for the significance of this anniversary celebration, for the opportunities to renew and strengthen relationships with you and one another and to reaffirm our commitments to both.

Because today is the first day of the rest of our lives, make us even more receptive to your leadership and guidance in the future than we have been before. Help us as individuals and as the ones who have covenanted to be _____ Church ever to remember that to be alive is to grow, and to grow is to change. Keep us faithful to the ties and traditions of the past that sustain, enrich, motivate, and challenge us. But free us from the chains of the past that make us complacent, unwilling to risk, afraid to be vulnerable. Enable us to live by the philosophy that what is past is prologue so we can face our tomorrows with openness and sensitivity—recognizing that we are responsible to share in the creation of our own and of our church's future. Amen.

C H U R C H   C E N T E N N I A L

God of the past, present, and future, unchanging and unchangeable throughout life's changes, we pause on this historic Sunday to sing and speak your praise. You are our help in ages past and our hope for years to come. You are our refuge and strength, a very present help in trouble. For your help and your presence within and among us, we are forever grateful.

We gather this day to thank you for the founders of and for our forebears in this church. For the gathering of this congregation and for the building of the structures in which we worship, learn, enjoy community, serve, and find ministry, each of us owes a debt of gratitude—a debt too often taken lightly or for granted, if thought about at all.

Forgive us for our insensitivity to the heritage we have been given, both spiritually and materially. Make us as concerned to grow and maintain our church in __ as were its members in __. As we today celebrate our past may we also rededicate ourselves to fulfilling our responsibilities of membership in our church, which are to live in all of our relationships according to the spirit and teachings of Jesus, to attend faithfully the services of worship of this church, to contribute as able to its support and to its benevolences, and to share as able in its organized work.

Hear this our Centennial prayer as well as the silent prayers we now offer. Amen.

Teacher Appreciation

Great Shepherd, who loves and cares for us as a shepherd cares for a flock, we pause to acknowledge and praise you for the fact that all of us—no matter who we are, whatever our race, religion, ethnicity, class, or sexual orientation; in spite of our faults and sinful ways—are a part of your flock. You have created us! We are yours! Thank you!

Forgive us for the times when we have strayed from your presence in words or deeds. And may our worship today inspire us to rededicate ourselves to follow you more faithfully and not to lose contact with your Holy Spirit. For you are the Ground of our Being, and in and from you we receive guidance and direction, strength to cope with whatever comes our way, and healing for the hurts that are a part of life.

We are especially grateful this day for those of our church who have been teaching these truths to our children and youth during this church school year. We thank you for their commitment and dedication to helping their students learn about our faith—a faith that always is only one generation away from extinction if it is not taught by and caught from us and others.

Hear these our prayers that are offered in the spirit of the One who also was like a shepherd to those who followed, even Jesus, the Christ. Amen.

MUSIC APPRECIATION

Creator God, the great Conductor of life's symphony who desires that we follow your direction, we pause to praise you for your majestic orchestration of the universe in which we live. You have given a rhythm, tempo, and beat to life that bring harmony to the ear when we follow the score before us. You cue us through difficult passages and make us feel secure in the knowledge that you can keep us and those near us together when the music is hard and the playing is rough.

We confess, however, that sometimes we fail to follow your leading. We let our eyes and minds drift from the podium. We become so intent on the notes we are playing and how we want to play them that we forget about you and the other symphony members who depend upon us and who are affected by our individualized and thus shoddy performance. So the notes we play become discordant and destroy the intonation life's music is meant to have. Or, failing to watch your baton, we find ourselves out of synchronization with you and the other players.

Forgive us, we pray. And may we rededicate ourselves this day to following more closely you who are our Conductor and Jesus, the Christ, our concertmaster, who has given us the note on which we are to tune the instrument we call life. Amen.

BIBLE PRESENTATION

God of every time and place, whom we have come to know through your still, small voice within us, through the marvels of nature, and through the ancient scriptures, we have come to worship you on this day when the importance of the Bible is recognized and affirmed. For the Bible, which is a lamp to our feet and a light to our paths, for the record of humanity's endeavors to understand your nature and how we human beings are to live, we offer our thanks. Today we recognize our gratitude to some of those whose writings and teachings have been preserved for posterity:

To Micah, who reminded us of what you require of us—to do justice, and to love kindness, and to walk humbly with you.

To Isaiah, who held out the hope for peace when he wrote, "The wolf shall live with the lamb, the leopard shall lie down with the kid, the calf and the lion and the fatling together."

To the psalmist, who taught that you are "our refuge and our strength, a very present help in trouble."

To Jesus, whose teachings remind us that when we feed the hungry, welcome the stranger, care for the sick, provide for people's basic needs—in other words, have compassion for others—we are loving and serving you.

To the many writers who remind us that you are Love.

O God, as we ponder your Word, may we, as James suggested, be not readers or hearers only, but doers, as was Jesus, the Christ, in whose spirit we pray. Amen.

CONGREGATIONAL MEETING

Creative Source of all being, whose ways, will, and love were personified in the life of Jesus of Nazareth whom we call the Christ because he was willing to live as a beacon whose light would attract people to you, we, your children, have come to rededicate and renew our lives in this hour of worship.

We gather as the church, members of a community of faith committed to being the body of Christ that tells the story and carries on the ministry of Jesus. We gather here in this sanctuary as a specific body, _____ of _____. We thank you for this community of people who have covenanted to love you with heart, soul, mind, and strength and our neighbor as ourselves and to carry on the work of the Christ in and through this local congregation.

We thank you, too, for this day on which we can discharge one of our responsibilities as members—that of reviewing, assessing, and expressing appreciation for the work accomplished in your name in the year just past and for the privilege of making decisions that will affect our future. May we as a church be even more what we are called to be: a sanctuary where we are fortified for the living of daily life, seekers who gather to learn more about you and ourselves, and a people who scatter to carry on your work and to be the church in our community and world. Amen.

A CLERGY STAFF PERSON'S FIRST SUNDAY

Infinite God, whom we have come to know most fully through Jesus, we gather as the church which is called to be the body of Christ at work in the world today, proclaiming the teachings and exemplifying the love of Jesus. For all who have been the church in ages past and who have told the old, old story of Jesus and his love, for all who are the church now and who strive to retell and relive that story, we offer our praise and gratitude.

This morning we thank you for your church that meets in this place to find inspiration, challenge, knowledge, wisdom, forgiveness, community, and channels for service. For its heritage of __ years and for those today who labor to keep alive and pass on this heritage, we bless your name.

We especially feel the presence of your Spirit in our worship as we welcome _____ into our church family. May (he/she/they) feel the warmth of your acceptance and love through us as (he/she/they) begin(s) a new chapter in (his/her/their) life (lives). And may our lives be fed and enriched by _____'s ministry to us.

Keep us ever aware of our calling to be a church, not a club; a sanctuary, but also a springboard for service; a community in which to share both joys and concerns; a family with which to have fun but also in which to find comfort and support. Let us never forget that the church is not a building, the church is not a program, but the church is a people—and we are the church! We pray in the spirit of the one who is the cornerstone of the church, Jesus, the Christ. Amen.

A CLERGY STAFF PERSON'S LAST SUNDAY

Sovereign God, changeless in our ever-changing world, the Constant to whom we always can turn and upon whom we always can rely; we pause in our busyness to reestablish conscious contact with you, the Ground of our Being.

We praise and thank you for all of your gifts, many of which we are aware, many of which we take for granted. One of your gifts to us of which we are poignantly mindful is the gift of our friend and loved one, _____, who lovingly, ably, and faithfully has ministered to and with us in recent years. For her/his friendship; for her/his words of challenge and inspiration from the pulpit; for her/his acts of pastoral care; for the teaching, leadership, and example she/he has provided for our youth; we thank you.

Grant, gracious God, that as _____ begins another ministry, she/he will do so assured of your continued presence and assured that she/he carries with her/him our love and best wishes. Thank you, God, for the fact that our lives have intersected. For we are the better and richer because our paths have crossed! Amen.

WHEN DISASTER STRIKES

Ever-present God, to have strike close to home disasters such as the _____ that devastated neighboring communities on _____ abruptly reminds us that none of us knows what this day or tomorrow holds for him or her or friends or neighbors. The same natural laws and processes that the vast majority of time result in happiness, health, and life are the same laws and processes that sometimes result in tragedy, illness, and death.

We pause today to recognize that we are finite and that although we have relatively little control over the quantity of our lives we have great control over the quality of our lives. Therefore, may we be concerned not only about how long we live but also with how we live.

We recognize, too, that life contains the difficult, the uncertain, and the unexpected. But life also contains the strength and constancy of your love and presence that do not remove obstacles but that enable us to cope with and get through them.

Thank you for life! Thank you for your love! Amen.

WHEN TRAGEDY OCCURS

Loving God, constant during the changes of life, our refuge during the storms of life, our strength in times of tragedy, our hope when we feel desolated and devastated, who does not desire or will that any of your children should perish, we gather this day as a congregation in special need. You know the shock and trauma that have been ours since learning of the tragic event that affects our church family. We cannot believe that _____ is dead, but we know that we must face the reality that no longer will she/he be physically present among us.

Compassionate God, we pray your blessing on all who grieve and suffer, all persons and families whose lives have been touched by death, especially _____. Motivate us to reach out and touch _____ and others so affected in some concrete, helpful way.

Enable us, too, to be more appreciatively of the life that is ours. Since we do not know what either the present or the future holds, may we use wisely each day that dawns. May we not pave our way with so many good intentions. Rather, stir us to speak those words of love and gratitude, to give those embraces of warmth and caring, to offer our apologies and forgiveness, to do those acts of kindness, now—not later. And with the poet Whittier, may we affirm:

"Within the maddening maze of things, when tossed by storm and flood,

   To one fixed trust my spirit clings; I know that God is good!

I know not where [God's] islands lift their fronded palms in air;

   I only know I cannot drift beyond [God's] love and care.

I know not what the future hath of marvel or surprise,

   Assured alone that life and death [God's] mercy underlies." Amen.

Prayers for Any Sunday

O God, our Eternal Contemporary, who loves us as a mother and father love their child, we pause in your presence with feelings of awe, gratitude, expectation, and at times even bewilderment. Because you are infinite there is much about you that we finite beings cannot comprehend. But because you are like a parent there is much about you that we can understand.

We know that you want for us the best but that at times you cannot prevent our experiencing the worst. We know that you want us to love and serve you but that we have the freedom to rebel against you. We know that you hurt and ache when we are experiencing pain or grief.

For loving us enough to let us be persons instead of puppets, for walking with us and holding our hands when life's roads are rocky or steep, for crying with us and rejoicing with us, accept our gratitude. Thank you, God, for being our Creator, our Guide, and our Friend. Amen.

Eternal One, we have come to worship and praise you for being all that you are.

You are Love. Because you love us we know that we are of value and worth. We are OK! Remind us again that our calling is to love you in return by sharing your love with others.

You are Truth. The meaning of life and the world is to be found in you. But we sometimes forget that you are

our God and we are your people. And we seek life's ultimate meaning in the lesser gods that sometimes beckon.

You are Forgiveness. When we confess our sins you
respond with your amazing grace that enables us to put
the past behind us and to begin again.

You are Strength. Your power is latent within us just
waiting to be tapped. To do so is to find that we are able
to do more than we realize or than we thought we could.
For this we are grateful.

You are Consolation. Hurt, pain, and despair seem
indigenous to our lives. But you directly, and indirectly
through our loved ones and friends, bring us comfort and
lead us through the shadows of life until we are back in
the sunlight again. Thank you!

We pray in the spirit of your incarnation, Jesus, the
Christ. Amen.

Well, God, another week has passed and a new one begins. So at this juncture we want to interrupt our personal, family, and business routines long enough to spend
a special hour with you and your friends. In fact, Creator
God, we do not view this hour as an interruption. Rather,
we feel it is vital to our lives. For here we are challenged
to think about a Supreme Being, not just lesser gods; ab-
solutes, not just relativities; ideals, not just ideas; persons,
not just things; quality of existence, not just quantity;
what is right, not just what is expedient.

So while we are here enable us to listen, to evaluate,
and to be motivated to leave this sanctuary and live this

new week in such a way that the Christ will be reflected
in our words and actions. Amen.

God of this and every day, the smell of the grass after
the rain, the iris blooming in our gardens, the singing of
the birds, the smiles on the faces of our families and
friends remind us of how great you are and how good life
is! So on this your day we have come into this setting to
acknowledge and praise you for your presence in our
world and in our lives. For it is your presence that enables
even storm clouds to have silver linings and that enables
us to find joy even in the midst of despair.

We thank you, Fountain of life, for our faith—a faith
that makes a difference in our lives. For ours is a faith
that provides an example and pattern for daily living.
Our faith challenges us to ponder the life and teachings of
Jesus and therein to find suggestions for our lives—such
as to love rather than hate, to serve rather than use, to be
involved rather than apathetic, to give as well as receive.

Today we profess this faith through the words we
speak and sing and by our presence here. Forbid that our
profession will cease at the conclusion of this hour.
Rather, may the reminder of today and this new week
find our professions translated into our actions as we go
about the living of each day. Amen.

Great, gracious, and giving God, we glorify you because
of who you are and whose we are. You are our Creator,
the ultimate Source of life and love and the other blessings we sometimes take for granted, such as the abilities

to see a waterfall, hear an infant, taste warm bread, touch an animal, and smell a rose. We have been created with a God-shaped vacuum within us, and we drift aimlessly and hopelessly on the sea of life until we invite your spirit to fill the vacuum, thereby giving us the buoyancy and stability needed for us to move toward the goals we have set.

For offering to bring our lives order from chaos, wholeness from fragmentation, hope from despair, forgiveness from guilt, self-worth from self-loathing, generosity from selfishness, caring from apathy; thank you, Redeeming One.

Walk with us as we enter this new week. By your grace enable us to see possibilities rather than problems, windows of opportunity rather than closed doors, persons rather than things, life rather mere existence. Amen.

Ever-calling, ever-beckoning God, who accepts us as we are but who also knows the persons we can become, we pause in our worship to share with you our feelings of gratitude, contrition, and resolve. We are grateful for your acceptance and love that enable us better to accept and love ourselves. For only when we do so can we accept and love others. We thank you as well for the other innumerable blessings we enjoy: family, friends, health, food, shelter, talents, church, nation, coping power.

When we reflect on who we are because of the gifts we enjoy we become more mindful of whose we are. Yet, we confess that too often we fail to live as though we are yours. Thus, for our willful sins and failures both of commission and omission as well as for our unthinking and unintentional wrongdoings, we ask your forgiveness.

May our having been in this place this morning and having shared in words and music that speak of you give us the resolve to enter this new week more sensitive to the fact that you have called us to be your children, your servants, and your witnesses. Although we are free to shut our ears to and turn our backs on your calling, may we, in love that is a response to your love for us, say, "Here am I, dear God, use me!" Amen.

O God, whose eye is always on the sparrow and on us because we are special and precious in your sight, we confess that our view of you and the world in which we live sometimes is warped and filtered by what we see through the eyes of ABC, CBS, NBC, CNN, and Fox. For so often these and other media deceive us into thinking that human life is cheap, that the end always justifies the means, that violent actions bring prompt results, and that more and bigger always are better.

Thus, we thank you for this hour and this place that help us put life back into proper perspective. For here we are confronted by your Word and reminded that our lives should be focused on what is true, honorable, just, pure, lovely, and gracious. Here we are reminded of and can feel again the strength with which you fill our lives— strength that enables us to cope with whatever comes our way.

Thank you for our church, loving God, because it calls us to worship you, refocus our lives, and then to

leave your sanctuary and go out to live the fully human
and humane life you have created us to live—a life pat-
terned after the one who knew you more completely and
saw you more clearly than has any other person—Jesus,
the Christ, our Savior. Amen.

Eternal God, who is One and Universal, Creator of all—
red and yellow, black, brown, and white—we pause to
worship and praise you. Loving God, you are known by
different names and worshiped in different ways. Yet, you
are the God of East and West, North and South.

We gather today to confess that we and others have
not been the best of your children. We have let race and
nationality and culture and sex and age and forms of gov-
ernment and the resources of our planet divide and create
barriers among us. We have forsaken the ancient teachings of the prophets Isaiah and Micah and continued to
rely on violence or warfare to settle our differences. You
forgiveness, therefore, is needed by all of us, wherever we
live in your world.

Gracious God, whom we have come to know and
love through the one who was called the Prince of Peace,
may negotiations occur so that lives will not be lost on
the battlefields, in the air, and in cities, towns, or villages
anywhere in the world due to war. For we know that you
desire that we love and have concern and compassion
even for those who may be our enemies.

As we pray for the needs of our world, we also pray
for the needs of our individual lives. Forgive our sins;
calm our anxieties; strengthen our resolve; keep us faith-

ful, hopeful, and helpful as we go about the living of this new week. We pray in the spirit of the one who said, "Lo, I am with you always." Amen.

Eternal, ever-present God, Creator of the world and giver of life to all who dwell therein, Parent of all nations and races, as the sun's warm rays call forth a blossom from a bud, so your still, small voice calls forth the best that is in us. Thus, this morning we pause in your presence—attracted by the warmth of your love and desiring to have our lives remolded so they better will fit into your will and ways.

Forgive us, gracious God, for forgetting that you can help us transform and remake our lives. Our hatred can be turned into love, our ingratitude into thanksgiving, our insensitivity into feeling and caring, our anxiety into confidence, our pessimism into optimism, our stress into release from tension, our intentions into deeds, our apathy into action, our parochialism into universal concern, our myopia into farsightedness, our prejudice into tolerance, our penchant for doing evil into a penchant for doing good.

Make us aware, therefore, of the areas of our lives in which changes are needed. And with your leading and inspiration, enable us to address ourselves to this task. Amen.

Eternal Spirit of the universe, who began the process of creation and thus is the source of our very lives, you who are to us like a loving father and a compassionate mother;

we your children pause in reverence to praise and thank you for the gift of life.

For talents to use, for the freedom to choose; for the capacity to cope, for the blessing of hope; for loved ones for whom we can care, for others with whom we can share; we express our gratitude.

We confess, O God, that at times—in fact, too often—we do not use our lives wisely. We let our talents rust or go to waste. We fracture relationships. We hurt others by what we do or say, or fail to say or do. We go against what our conscience tells us is right. We are myopic, thinking only of ourselves or our immediate world. We selfishly accumulate but do not give out of gratitude to those whose need is apparent.

Forgive us, forgiving God. And on this, the first day of the rest of our lives, help us to begin to right the wrongs and repair the damages that have created barriers between ourselves and you and ourselves and others. Thus, gracious God, our prayer at the beginning of this new day and week is that we will be better children of yours and better brothers and sisters of one another. Amen.

Let us now join hands and hearts together and share in the prayer that Jesus has taught our family OUR FATHER. . . .